THE FRANKFURT COOKBOOK

*"To those he loves, God gives a home
and sustenance in Frankfurt."*

*Johann Hermann Dielhelm
(c. 1710 - 1784)*

D1337810

© 2009 Verlag Gebrüder Kornmayer, Germany
http://www.kornmayer-verlag.de
ISBN 978-3-938173-78-7

Autoren: Linda White und Evert Kornmayer
Grußwort: Petra Roth, Oberbürgermeisterin der
Stadt Frankfurt am Main
Satz/Layout: Gebrüder Kornmayer
Bilder: Evert Kornmayer
Druck: leibi, Neu-Ulm

Deutsche Bibliothek - CIP-Einheitsaufnahme. Ein Titel-
satz dieser Publikation ist bei der Deutschen Bibliothek (Frankfurt) erhältlich.

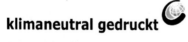

klimaneutral gedruckt

376-53247-0509-1007
weitere Infos: www.leibi.de/klima

LINDA WHITE & EVERT KORNMAYER

THE FRANKFURT COOKBOOK

The best recipes from Mainhattan

VERLAG GEBRÜDER KORNMAYER

Petra Roth

Salutation

The Frankfurt kitchen has often been described and praised. Even Goethe's mother, Frau Rat, referred to the fine art of cooking. "I have no fear of princes, I can cook!" she said spiritedly when her son visited Frankfurt in the company of the Duke of Weimar. The first books of culinary specialties of the Free Imperial City appeared more than 150 years ago. Naturally they included recipes for the best-known Frankfurt dishes such as Frankfurters, Green Sauce and the Frankfurt Crown.

Of course, the culinary arts continually developed. Just as Frankfurt is a lively city where many cultures and influences meet, the Frankfurt kitchen is also extremely varied. It always has a suitable locality for its multicultural residents. In no other city is it possible to get to know so many different nationalities by way of their food, and thus to constantly experience something new. For example, visitors to the Book Fair or the IAA – International Automobile Exhibition – can always find a Frankfurt resident eager to introduce them to their cuisine.

It is just these influences that influence Frankfurt's specialties today and will continue to do so in the future. Nevertheless, it is always interesting to rediscover the originals. That is possible with this new cookbook from the Verlag Gebrüder Kornmayer. The Frankfurt Cookbook presents a connection between old favorites and new recipes. It also gives even Frankfurt citizens a completely new glimpse of their regional kitchen.

Petra Roth
Lord Mayor
of the City of Frankfurt am Main

Table of Contents

The „Römer" (town hall)

Frankfurt is the Cradle of the Culinary Arts in Germany

Its repute starts with its specialties. We can think of no other city that is so well known worldwide as Frankfurt for its Frankfurters. But other tasty specialties got their start here, too: Frankfurt Kranz (a cake in the shape of a crown), Frankfurt Brenten (a marzipan confection similar to Bethmännchen which also originated in Frankfurt) and Frankfurt Brühwurst (boiled sausage). However, when one thinks of Frankfurt and food, one immediately thinks of Frankfurt Green Sauce – particularly with boiled potatoes. And truly, when it is well made it is something of a sensation.

Sometimes Frankfurt is called "Mainhattan" – a play on its location on the Main River and its skyscrapers reminiscent of Manhattan. The name refers not just its banking quarter, but also to the pulsing rhythm of the city – its shopping streets, its bars, discos and exclusive clubs. It's where international meets village; many languages are spoken here but there are nooks and crannies that have come directly out of Grimms' Fairy Tales. Respite from the city hectic is also just a step away on the river. River cruises are available, and a ferry crosses between Schwanheim and Höchst. The Main flows slowly here, setting the mood for a stroll or a picnic. Upstream, you can stop at a house-boat pub or try the fare at Ma Chance or the Gerbermühle, a former mill that has been turned into a restaurant and hotel.

That's Frankfurt's own special character. What other city has its own Fressgass' – a real epicures' street? It is no coincidence that the Fressgass' is adjacent to the

Typical restaurant near to the Main River

noble Westend, Frankfurt's banking- and bourgeois quarter. You can shop in the many bakeries, butcher shops and delicatessens along this street. Its traditional restaurants attracted and still attract the crème de la crème of the city, and people come from far and wide to its wine festivals.

The wine festivals on the Fressgass' and in other parts of the city feature the famous grape wines from all over Germany, but Frankfurt has its own "national" drink as well – apple wine, a version of cider. You don't have to wait for a festival to enjoy it. Both locals and visitors feel at home in the apple wine pubs, found particularly in Sachsenhausen. A few are Wagner, the Affentor-Schänke, Zum Gemalten Haus, Dauth-Schneider, Apfelwein Klaus and the Kanonesteppel. Across the Main River from Sachsenhausen are the Friedberger Warte and Mütter Ernst.

They specialize in the tart drink, served in special "quilted pattern" glasses or in grey-and-blue pitchers, called Bembel. Apple wine is refreshing served cold mixed with mineral water – gespritzt – in summer, or hot with a bit of sugar in winter.

The people of Frankfurt have always known how to enjoy food. A special place for sightseeing and enjoying is the Kleinmarkthalle in the old part of town. On work days, all sorts of food – from Green Sauce to caviar – as well as flowers and seed, are sold at more than 150 stands on about 16,000 square feet of space. Some stands overflow with fresh fruit, vegetables and meat from the region; others specialize in imports from Italy, Greece, Turkey, the Middle East, the Far East and Latin America.

In addition to the market hall, a number of colorful outdoor farmers' markets featuring local and regional

Apple-Wine-Pub „Zum Gemalten Haus"

products are held in Frankfurt's various neighborhoods one or two days each week. Among the larger markets in the center city are the Konstablermarkt at the Konstablerwache square on Thursdays and Saturdays and the Schillermarkt along the Schillerstraße on Fridays.

The markets are a real cornucopia of food from the environs; vegetables – particularly potatoes and asparagus – grow in the Rhine flatlands to the south of Frankfurt. The Taunus mountains provide game and fish; wine comes from the slopes of the Rheingau. The Wetterau is known for its fruit and grain and Rhön lambs have been a delicacy for as long as anyone can remember.

Besides those open to the public, two major wholesale markets are located in Frankfurt: the Großmarkthalle – Europe's largest transshipment center for food – and the Airport, the site of one of Europe's biggest fish markets.

These markets are direct descendants of the Frankfurt Trade Fair. Of course, all manner of consumer goods have been traded here ever since 1227, and food was a natural appendage. Today the Fairs are devoted to books, automobiles or household goods. About 50 take place each year, attracting more than 2.6 million visitors – be sure to make restaurant reservations well in advance when a fair is going on.

On the following pages, you can find inspiration – or better, try out the recipes! You will see, it is not really difficult and it's fun. And it's also not forbidden to drink one or three glasses of wine – whether from Frankfurt's own Lorberg vineyard or from one of its apple-wine cellars.

Measuring Units & Amounts

In our experience, ingredient amounts and cooking time can be given only in approximation. The characteristics of ingredients vary from one place to another and the conditions of kitchens – from pans to ovens – differ greatly. This, along with individual taste and preference, calls for tasting and adjustment by the cook. With all recipes, everyone should use his or her own experience in the preparation of dishes.

Abbreviations used in this book:

lb   = pound
oz   = ounce
c   = cup
t   = teaspoon
T   = tablespoon

Other Measurements:

Pinch = The amount you can pick up between thumb and forefinger
Pkg   = Package
°F   = Degrees Fahrenheit (212°F = 100°C)

Snacks

FRANKFURTERS
FRANKFURTER WÖRSCHTSCHE

Frankfurters are well known all over the world. Those who argue that they are Vienna sausage will be disappointed: the sausage from Vienna is an offspring of the Frankfurt prototype: Frankfurter Würstchen have been known in Frankfurt am Main since the 13th century. However, they did earn their world fame with a detour by way of Vienna. Starting about 1805, a butcher from Frankfurt, Johann Georg Lahner, made and sold Frankfurters there.

Frankfurters are also known as hot dogs in the USA, but real Frankfurters from Frankfurt are longer and slimmer. The city is also home of a well-known beef sausage – Gref-Völsings Rindswurst – which had its beginnings in the large Jewish community here and which is still produced locally according to the traditional recipe. Many prominent Jewish families – Rothschild, Oppenheim, Speyer – lived for generations in Frankfurt and played an important role in its history and daily life. Much of the German-Jewish spirit was lost in the Holocaust, but today a prosperous Jewish community is once again contributing to the cosmopolitan air of the city.

SERVES 1:
2 frankfurters (hot dogs)
Water

ACCOMPANIMENTS:
Prepared mustard
Potato salad, buttered bread or buns

PREPARATION:
In a large pan, bring to the boil enough water to cover the Frankfurters well. Remove from heat, put the Frankfurters into the water and allow to sit 6 to 8 minutes. Remove from the water and serve with desired accompaniments.

COUNTRY CHEESE WITH MUSIC

HANDKÄS´ MIT MUSIK

The word Handkäs´ comes from the original method of making this cheese, because it was shaped by hand. Handkäs' mit Musik is not eaten with a fork. Simply cut a slice with a knife, pick it up with the point of the knife and put the bite in your mouth. Alternately, put a slice of Handkäs' on a piece of bread, with the knife add a bit of the "music" and take a bite. The "music" refers to the sounds that result from the process of digesting the raw onion.

SERVES 2:
4 Handkäs', about 3½ to 5 oz each (or substitute Münster, Limburger or other low-fat, raw-milk cheese)

THE MUSIC:
½ c vinegar
¼ c oil
¼ c water
Salt
Freshly-ground black pepper
3 onions, diced
Cumin seed

FOR SERVING:
Brown bread
Butter

PREPARATION:
For the marinade, mix the vinegar, oil and water in a small bowl. Salt and pepper to taste, then add the diced onions and sprinkle with the cumin seed. Spoon the

marinade evenly over the rounds of cheese and allow to sit one or two hours. Serve with brown bread and butter, and apple wine or beer to drink.

SACHSENHAUSEN SNOW FLURRY

SACHSENHÄUSER SCHNEEGESTÖBER

Sachsenhausen is well known for its apple-wine pubs. Visitors to Frankfurt are particularly attracted to the area known as Alt (Old)-Sachsenhausen because of its concentration of restaurants and pubs.

SERVES 4:
2 small rounds (about 7 oz each) of Camembert cheese
7 oz Philadelphia cream cheese
3 T butter, softened
2 onions, diced
2 pinches of black pepper
Freshly-ground white pepper to taste
Chopped parsley

PREPARATION:
Place the Camembert, cream cheese and butter in a bowl. Mash with a fork and mix well. Stir in the onion and add pepper to taste. Garnish with a little parsley and serve with farmers' bread and butter.

Soup

FRANKFURT LENTIL SOUP
FRANKFURTER LINSENSUPPE

Once upon a time, at noon on Saturdays the scent of lentil soup wafted over all of Frankfurt. Superstitious people ate up all their lentil soup on New Year's Day so they would have enough money the entire year – but maybe it was just because the soup tastes so good.

SERVES 4:
7 oz dried lentils
4 cups water
1 T butter
1 T flour
2 pieces salt pork, cooked
3½ oz sauerkraut
Salt
½ c sour cream

PREPARATION:
Soak the lentils in water about 2 hours, then rinse several times in a sieve and place over a saucepan to drip. Place the lentils in the saucepan, fill with water to cover and cook until tender but not too soft. Melt the butter, stir in the flour and add to the soup, mixing well. Cut the salt pork into pieces, add to the soup and simmer another 20 minutes. Cut the sauerkraut into fine strips, add to the lentils and salt to taste. Spoon the hot soup into bowls, dot with two tablespoons of sour cream and serve with farmers' bread.

FRANKFURT POTATO SOUP

FRANKFURTER KARTOFFELSUPP´

This is a hearty potato soup made with Frankfurters; it can be enhanced with pieces of bacon.

SERVES 6:
1¾ lb mealy-cooking potatoes
4 cups chicken stock
1 leek
1 T butter
½ onion, chopped
1 T Green-sauce herbs, chopped
⅓ cup cream
1 t marjoram
1 t dry mustard
Pinch of nutmeg
Salt
6 Frankfurters

PREPARATION:
Peel and cube the potatoes, place in a boiler with the chicken stock and cook until the potatoes are soft. Slice the leek into small strips. Melt the butter in a casserole dish, add the leek, onion and Green-sauce herbs and cook until the onions are translucent but not brown. Combine the mixture with the potatoes and puree into a soup. Stir in the cream and correct the seasoning with the marjoram, mustard, nutmeg and salt. Cut the Frankfurters into small pieces, place in the soup and warm 5 minutes. Serve hot.

Meat Dishes

CUTLETS WITH SAUERKRAUT

RIPPCHEN MIT KRAUT

In Frankfurt, Rippsche is a cured pork cutlet. It may be served cold or slightly warmed on top of the sauerkraut, accompanied by farmers' bread and mustard.

SERVES 4:
1 small apple
1 32-oz jar of sauerkraut
1 onion, diced
2 bay leaves
6 juniper berries
½ c apple wine (cider)
4 pork cutlets

PREPARATION:
Peel and core the apple and cut into thin slices. Put the sauerkraut in a saucepan and add the apple slices, onion, bay leaves and juniper berries. Mix well and add the apple wine. Place the cutlets on the sauerkraut. Cook, covered, over low heat for about 40 minutes. Serve on a warm plate with mashed potatoes.

BOILED BEEF WITH GREEN SAUCE

TAFELSPITZ MIT GRÜNER SOSSE

Tafelspitz is the tapered, tender tail of beef. To keep it juicy, have the water at a rolling boil before putting in the meat.

SERVES 10:
1 small leek stalk
1 onion
3 or 4 carrots, diced
1 small slice celeriac, diced
1 bay leaf
A few peppercorns
Salt
4½ lbs prime-beef filet
Boiled potatoes
Green Sauce (see recipe)

PREPARATION:
Slice the leek in half vertically. Halve the onion and place it cut side down in a large saucepan without oil. Add the vegetables, bay leaf and seasonings along with enough water to cover the meat. Do not cover the boiler. Bring to the boil and add the meat. Cook a few minutes, skimming the foam off the top, then reduce the heat and simmer 2½ to 3 hours. Remove the meat from the liquid. Cut across the grain into ¼-inch-thick slices and arrange on a plate with the boiled potatoes. Spoon the green sauce over the meat and potatoes.

GOETHE'S GRANDMOTHER'S HAMBURGER STEAK

FRIKADELLEN NACH ART VON GOETHES GROSSMUTTER

Many recipes were found in the estate of Anna Margaretha Justina Lindheimer, the grandmother of Johann Wolfgang von Goethe. Among them was the following recipe for hamburger steak. The ingredients are those listed in 1724; the amounts come from current recipes.

SERVES 4:
¼ lb thick-sliced bacon
1 lb ground beef
2 eggs
½ c fine bread crumbs
1 T lemon juice
Salt to taste
½ t ground cloves
Pinch of ground nutmeg
½ t freshly-grated ginger
Oil for frying

PREPARATION:
Finely dice the bacon and in a bowl mix well with the ground beef. Mix in the eggs and bread crumbs and allow to stand 5 minutes. Stir in the lemon juice, salt and spices, and let stand another 5 minutes. Stir the mixture once more, then form patties by hand. Heat the oil in a skillet and cook the patties at medium heat until cooked through. The hamburger steaks taste particularly good with potato salad or home fries.

SACHSENHAUSEN BREWER'S BEEF GOULASH

RINDERGULASCH NACH ART DER SACHSENHÄUSER BRAUMEISTER

The company history of the Henninger Brewery began in 1655 in the city of Frankfurt, to which it gave not only its Kaiser Pilsner beer but also its landmark, the Henninger Tower.

SERVES 5:
¼ lb salt pork
3 T butter
1¾ lb onions, sliced
2¼ lb lean beef, cubed
1 bouquet garni
2 T flour
1⅔ c water
1 c beef broth
½ bottle beer
2 cloves of garlic, pressed
1 t sugar
1 T vinegar
Salt
Freshly-ground black pepper
1 T chopped parsley

PREPARATION:
Cut the salt pork into small cubes and brown in a skillet. Remove the cubes and reserve the fat. Melt the butter in the skillet and cook the onion slices in it until they are translucent but not brown. Set the onions

aside. Place a little of the reserved fat and the cubed beef to the skillet. Brown the beef, then place it along with the bouquet garni in a Dutch oven. Put the remaining reserved fat into the skillet. Stir in the flour, add the water and cook over low heat until the gravy turns golden. Remove from heat and stir in the beef broth and beer, mixing until smooth. Return to heat and bring to a boil. When the sauce is thick, add the garlic, sugar and vinegar. Cook about 3 minutes, then correct the seasoning with salt and pepper. Sprinkle the onion over the pieces of meat and pour the gravy over it. Cover and cook in a preheated 350°F oven about 1½ hours. Add a little more beer if needed during cooking. Before serving, remove the bouquet garni and sprinkle the meat with the salt pork pieces and chopped parsley. Serve with Frankfurt Potato Dumplings and a glass of beer.

GREENBACK

RINDERLENDE MIT KRÄUTERKUSTE

A greenback in Frankfurt is not necessarily a U.S. dollar, even though dollars are no stranger in the banking quarter. In the kitchen, it is a strip of sirloin cooked in an herb crust – an edible greenback.

SERVES 4:
1 lb sirloin (alternative: loin of pork)
¼ lb sausage meat
Oil
70 g chopped Green-sauce herbs (parsley, sorrel,
   cress, chives, burnet, borage, chervil)
   (alternative: 1 twig fresh sage and
   1 bunch coriander)
¼ c Parmesan cheese
Salt and pepper to taste

MARINADE:
Olive oil
1 clove of garlic, pressed

PREPARATION:
To make the marinade, mix the olive oil and garlic. Brush the marinade over the sirloin, place the meat in a dish, cover and allow to sit in a cool place one or two days. Remove from the dish, pat dry and season with salt and pepper to taste. Heat the oil in a pan and brown the meat on all sides. Remove from the pan and cool. Finely chop the herbs. Grate the cheese; mix it with the sausage meat and chopped herbs. Place the mixture on the top side of the sirloin and press firmly. Put the meat in a grill pan and cook in a preheated 360°F oven for 25 minutes. For well-done beef, cook

another 5 minutes. Remove from oven and set in a warm place to rest a few minutes before slicing. Serve with seasonal vegetables and salad.

Fish Dishes

MAIN RIVER FISHERMAN'S STEW

MAINFISCHER-TOPF

The most famous Frankfurt fish can be found fossilized in the city's Senckenberg Museum. Only a few people know that Europe's third-largest fish market lies not on the coast but at the Frankfurt Airport. And once upon a time the Fishermen's Guilds in Frankfurt and Sachsenhausen owned the fishing rights on the Main River all the way from the Rhine to Aschaffenburg.

SERVES 4:

1¾ lb mixed fish (for example, barbell, bream, pike, carp and pikeperch), ready to cook
2 onions, cut into rings
1 bunch of soup vegetables, chopped
4 potatoes, cubed
1 clove of garlic, diced
1 t prepared mustard
Sea salt to taste
1 T vinegar
1 bay leaf
2 T Green-sauce herbs, chopped (parsley, sorrel, cress, chives, burnet, borage, chervil) (alternative: parsley)
6 c water
2 T butter
¾ c cream
Parsley to garnish
1 loaf French bread

PREPARATION:
Slice the fish into pieces about 2½ inches wide. Place the onions, soup vegetables, potatoes, garlic, mustard, salt, vinegar and herbs in a large pan of boiling water. Cover and simmer 20 minutes. Add the butter and cream and puree the mixture. Add the pieces of fish and allow to sit 5 to 8 minutes. Season to taste with salt and pepper. Place in soup bowls, garnish with parsley and serve with toasted French bread.

CARP IN GREEN SAUCE
KARPFEN IN GRÜNER SOSSE

This is a recipe from the "Practical Frankfurt Cookbook" published in 1877. This green sauce is a roux made with herbs.

SERVES 4:
1 carp
2 onions, sliced
1 bay leaf
3 cloves
Salt
Freshly-ground black pepper

SAUCE:
1 T flour
1 T butter
2 handsful each of parsley and chervil, finely chopped
Salt
Lemon juice to taste

PREPARATION:
Clean the carp and place in a pan with water. Add the onion, bay leaf, cloves and a little salt and pepper. Cook 20 to 30 minutes on low heat. In another pan, brown the flour, add the butter and stir. Pour the liquid from the fish into the second pan, straining through a sieve. Mix well with a wire whisk. Add the herbs and correct the seasoning with salt and lemon juice. Place the carp in a deep bowl and pour the sauce over it. Serve with boiled potatoes.

Vegetable Dishes

GREEN SAUCE WITH EGGS AND POTATOES

GRÜNE SOSSE MIT EI UND KARTOFFELN

This Frankfurt classic that features the famous Green Sauce (Grie Soß, as it's called in the local dialect) is popular all over the state of Hessen and beyond.

SERVES 4:
2¼ lb potatoes, cubed
8 eggs, hard cooked, peeled and halved vertically
Green Sauce (see recipe)

PREPARATION:
Wash the potatoes and cook in water about 20 minutes or until done. Drain. Serve with the eggs and green sauce.

SACHSENHAUSEN BAKERY POTATOES

SACHSENHÄUSER BÄCKERKARTOFFELN

A classic side-dish, this is a modified version of gratin potatoes. In the spring of 1589, Carolus Clusius planted the first potatoes in Germany in his Frankfurt garden – but only for the beauty of their blossoms. He was a botanist.

SERVES 4-6:
2 T shortening
2 onions, chopped
Butter for the casserole dish
2¼ lb potatoes, peeled and thinly sliced
Salt
Freshly-ground black pepper
Pinch of ground nutmeg
3 eggs
¾ c cream

PREPARATION:
Heat the shortening in a pan and cook the onions in it until they are translucent but not brown. Butter a casserole dish, place the onions and potato slices in it and season with the salt, pepper and nutmeg. In a bowl, mix the eggs and cream and pour over the potato mixture. Cook in a preheated 400°F oven 50 minutes or until golden brown on top.

FRANKFURT POTATO SALAD

FRANKFURTER KARTOFFELSALAT

Ideal with Frankfurters or hamburger steak.

SERVES 10:
3½ to 4 lb potatoes
¼ lb lean cured thick-sliced bacon, cubed
¼ lb onions, chopped
1 c beef broth
2 egg yolks
¼ c oil
⅓ c vinegar
Salt and freshly-ground black pepper to taste
Chives

PREPARATION:
Wash and cook the potatoes. Drain and peel while hot. Finely slice the lukewarm potatoes. Brown the bacon cubes and place over the potatoes, along with the fat. Sprinkle the onion over the mixture. Stir 3 tablespoons of the beef broth into the egg yolks. Heat the remaining broth and stir in oil, vinegar, salt and pepper. Stir in the potatoes and egg mixture and mix well. Garnish with chopped chives. Serve warm.

FRANKFURT POTATO DUMPLINGS

FRANKFURTER KARTOFFELKLÖSSE

This is a recipe from the "Frankfurt Cookbook" (1877) by Wilhelmine Rührig. The dumplings are served with goose, goulash or pork roast.

SERVES 6:
2¼ lb mealy-cooking potatoes
3 eggs
4 T butter
3 heaping T flour
Milk as needed
1 pinch nutmeg
Salt

GARNISH:
1 T butter
1 slice black bread, crumbled
or 1 onion, chopped

PREPARATION:
The day before, cook the potatoes until they are firm but not soft. Pour away the water and let the potatoes cool. The next day, peel the potatoes, grate them and mix with the remaining ingredients. Using your hands, form round dumplings from the potato mixture. In a large saucepan, bring lightly-salted water to the boil, add the dumplings, reduce heat and simmer 20 minutes. Drain and place the dumplings in a bowl. For the garnish, heat the butter in a pan, add bread crumbs or onion and cook until lightly browned. Pour over the dumplings and serve.

GOURMET SAUERKRAUT

FEINES SAUERKRAUT

The original Frankfurt kitchen requires that the sauerkraut be prepared the day before serving.

SERVES 4:
1 32-oz can wine sauerkraut
2 T clarified butter
1 onion, sliced
⅓ c beef broth
¼ c water
2 cloves
1 bay leaf
4 juniper berries
1 pinch sugar
Salt
Freshly-ground black pepper

PREPARATION:
Place the sauerkraut in a sieve, rinse with cold water and allow to drain well. Heat the clarified butter in a saucepan, add the onion and cook until translucent but not brown. Add the sauerkraut. Pour in the broth and water. Tie the spices in a spice bag and add to the mixture. Add the sugar, salt and pepper. Cover and simmer 30 minutes. Let stand overnight; reheat before serving.

Sauces

GREEN SAUCE
GRÜNE SOSSE

Even though the word "sauce" sounds more elegant, this "Original Frankfurt Dish" is always written the traditional way – Grüne Soße. The letter "ß" is a form of double-S, pronounced "SZ." The tradition is so deeply-rooted in the city on the Main that some people believe Gründonnerstag ("Green Thursday," that is, Maundy Thursday) gave its name to Green Sauce because it was always eaten on that day.

SERVES 4:
2 eggs
½ c chopped Green-sauce herbs (parsley, sorrel,
   cress, chives, burnet, borage, chervil)
2 egg yolks
2 T prepared mustard
2 T white-wine vinegar
½ c oil
1 c sour cream
Freshly-ground white pepper
Salt

PREPARATION:
Hard-cook the two eggs in boiling water, about 8 minutes. Cool under running water, peel and chop. Wash and dry the herbs, remove the stems and finely chop. Stir the egg yolks and mustard together in a bowl. Add the vinegar. Add the oil in a stream very slowly, beating continuously, to make a mayonnaise. Mix well with the sour cream. Stir in the chopped egg and herbs. Salt and pepper to taste. Serve the Green Sauce with hard-boiled eggs or beef.

APPLE-WINE SAUCE

APFELWEINSOSSE

This sauce is good not only on apple strudel but also on pancakes or as accompaniment to pork cutlets with prunes.

SERVES 4:
1½ c apple wine (cider)
½ c water
½ c sugar
3 T + 1 t corn starch
4 eggs, separated

PREPARATION:
In a large saucepan, bring the apple wine, water and sugar to the boil, stirring until the sugar is dissolved. Remove from heat. Dissolve the starch in a little cold water and mix well with the apple wine mixture. Return to heat and bring once more to a boil, stirring constantly. Reduce the heat and continue to cook, stirring constantly, until the sauce thickens. Remove from heat. In a small bowl, slightly beat the egg yolks, mix with about a tablespoon of the sauce and then add the remaining sauce, stirring constantly so the eggs don't scramble. In a separate bowl, beat the egg whites until stiff. Fold into the sauce. Refrigerate until well-cooled before serving.

Dessert

FRANKFURT AMBROSIA
FRANKFURTER GÖTTERSPEISE

A favorite of young and old.

SERVES 4:
4 eggs, separated
½ c sugar
2 c apple wine (cider) or apple juice
1½ pkg powdered gelatin
1 c cream

PREPARATION:
Separate the eggs and in a bowl stir the yolks with the sugar until they foam. Slowly add the apple wine, mixing well. Dissolve the gelatin in a little apple wine and add to the egg mixture. Beat the egg whites until stiff and in a separate bowl whip the cream. When the egg-yolk mixture begins to thicken, fold in first the whipped cream, then the egg whites. Refrigerate several hours before serving.

APPLE-WINE ICE CREAM
APFELWEIN-EIS

The Frankfurt poet Friedrich Stoltze rendered homage to apple wine in Frankfurt dialect thus: "dem Apfelwein: E wahrer Göttertroppe, Reweblut von Äppelbääm".
(Apple wine: a true drop of the gods, grape blossoms from an apple tree.) This is a traditional recipe with a special taste of apple wine and egg. Incidentally, an early energy drink was a mixture of apple wine, egg yolks and sugar.

SERVES 8:
1½ quarts apple wine (cider)
1 stick cinnamon
1 clove
1 bay leaf
2 c sugar
¼ c butter
2 vanilla beans
10 egg yolks

PREPARATION:
Place ⅔ of the apple wine along with the cinnamon, clove and bay leaf in a large boiler and on medium heat reduce to about half a quart. Remove from heat and add the remaining apple wine. In a double boiler, heat the sugar, butter and vanilla to 150°F. Stir in the egg yolks, then add the apple wine, pouring through a sieve. Heat to 175°F, stirring constantly. Place in an ice bath and cool to 150°F. Pour the mixture through a sieve, place in an ice cream machine and freeze according to machine instructions.

FRANKFURT APPLE CASSEROLE
FRANKFURTER APFELAUFLAUF

This is a classic that can be served as a main dish.

SERVES 4:
⅓ c raisins
Apple wine (cider) or water to cover
4 c milk
¾ c semolina
¼ c butter
Salt
½ c sugar
1 t vanilla extract
2¼ lb apples
½ c apple wine (cider)   VANILLA SAUCE:
Juice of 1 lemon   1 vanilla bean
4 eggs, separated   2 c milk
¼ c cream   3 T sugar
2–3 T cinnamon sugar   4–5 egg yolks

PREPARATION:
For the vanilla sauce, slice the vanilla bean in half lengthwise and scrape out the pulp. Place the vanilla bean and pulp with the milk and sugar in a saucepan and bring to the boil. Remove from heat, allow to stand 20 minutes and then remove the vanilla bean. Lightly beat the egg yolks into the milk mixture. Heat the sauce again but do not boil, stirring constantly, until it thickens. Place in the refrigerator to cool.
For the apple casserole, place the raisins in a large bowl, add apple wine or water and soak for 30 minutes. Pour the milk into a saucepan and bring to the boil.

Stir in the semolina, butter, salt, 3 T of the sugar and the vanilla extract. Reduce heat to low and cook until the semolina swells, about 10 minutes. Peel and core the apples and cut into thin slices. Place the apples in a bowl and add the apple wine, lemon juice and the remaining sugar. Drain the raisins, cut into small pieces and add to the apple mixture. Separate the eggs and beat the whites until stiff. In another bowl, mix the egg yolks and the cream. Add both mixtures to the semolina. Fold in the apple mixture. Butter a casserole dish, pour in the mixture and smooth the top. Bake in preheated 375°F oven about 45 minutes. Remove from oven and sprinkle with cinnamon sugar.

Confections

BETHMÄNNCHEN
BETHMÄNNCHEN

This is a Frankfurt original that is eaten not only at Christmastime. The tasty marzipan tidbits decorated with almond slices were created by the Bethmann banking family here. Originally, four almond slices represented the four sons of the family. After one of the sons died, each marzipan ball was decorated with only three slices – and so it remains today. The name is attributed to Napoleon, who during a stay in the Bethmann house said, "Give me another of those little Bethmännchen!"

Johann Wolfgang von Goethe also enjoyed them. Every Christmas, his mother sent him a package of Bethmännchen to Weimar.

FOR 60 PIECES:
1 lb raw marzipan
⅔ c powdered sugar, sifted
4½ oz ground blanched almonds
2 T flour, sifted
2 egg whites
180 blanched-almond halves

BEFORE BAKING:
2 egg yolks, lightly beaten with a little water

AFTER BAKING:
¼ c sugar
¼ c rose water

PREPARATION:
In a large bowl, mix together the raw marzipan, powdered sugar, ground almonds, flour and egg whites. Dampen your hands to keep the dough from sticking

to them; with the palms of your hands form small balls of 1- to 1½-inch diameter. There should be about 60 balls. Press 3 almond slices at regular intervals on the outside of each ball. Place the balls on two baking sheets lined with baking parchment and brush with the beaten egg yolks. Bake in a pre-heated 300°F oven about 15 minutes. Remove from the oven just as they begin to brown, otherwise they will be bitter. Bring the sugar and rose water to the boil and brush the mixture over the Bethmännchen while they are still hot.

FRANKFURT MOLDED MARZIPAN

FRANKFURTER BRENTEN

Brenten, a typically-Frankfurt confection, are formed in special molds and were one of Goethe's favorite treats.

SERVES 8:
1 c finely-ground almonds
¼ c rose water
2½ c powdered sugar
1 egg white
1½ T flour
Sugar

PREPARATION:
Place the almonds in a saucepan. Stir in the rose water and powdered sugar. Stir constantly over low heat until the mixture feels dry. Remove from heat and allow to sit overnight. Beat the egg white until stiff and fold, along with the flour, into the almond mixture. Knead a couple of times. Spread sugar on a dough board, place the dough on top of it and roll out to about ¼-inch thick. Flour a special brenten mold and press it firmly into the dough. (Alternately, use a cookie cutter.) Remove the mold and cut away the dough from the edges to make neat dough shapes. Cover a baking sheet with baking parchment, place the Brenten pieces on it and allow to dry 3 hours. Bake in a preheated 300°F oven 20 to 25 minutes or until done.

An easy alternative is to knead together 14 oz raw marzipan and 2 c powdered sugar, then continue as above, starting by beating the egg white.

FRANKFURT CROWN

FRANKFURTER KRANZ

The Frankfurt Crown is a cake that originated in the city on the Main River. It tastes best when baked the day before it is eaten.

FOR 1 CAKE:
DOUGH:
½ c butter
⅔ c sugar
4 eggs
Zest of ½ lemon
1 c corn starch
¾ c flour, 1 pinch salt
1 t baking powder

CREAM:
1 pkg dry vanilla
   pudding mix
2 c milk
½ c sugar
1¼ c butter
2 T cherry brandy

DECORATION:
1 T butter
¾ c sugar
2 c almond slivers
7 candied cherries, halved

PREPARATION:
Place the butter, sugar, eggs and lemon zest in a large bowl and beat by hand until the sugar is well incorporated. In another bowl, mix the corn starch, flour, baking powder and salt and add to the egg mixture. Butter and dust with flour a wreath-shaped cake pan (a Bundt pan will do). Pour in the batter and bake in a preheated 350°F oven 50 minutes. Remove from oven and cool for several hours. Cut twice through the cake to make 3 (or 4) layers. Make a cream of the pudding

mix, milk and sugar, cooking according to instructions on the packet. When done, remove from heat and cool, stirring occasionally. Cream the butter with a hand mixer. Stir the pudding into the butter by the tablespoonful. Add the cherry brandy and mix well. Spread ⅔ of the cream on the bottom two layers of the cake that have been cut apart and place the layers back together, coating the outside with a thin layer of the cream. For the decoration, in a saucepan heat the butter and sugar until it turns light brown. Stir in the almonds and spread the mixture as evenly as possible on a piece of buttered aluminum foil. Allow to cool. Remove this from the foil, finely chop with a knife and sprinkle over the wreath. Use the remaining ⅓ of the cream to form rosettes on the cake and gar- nish them with the cherry halves.

PRUNE SHEET CAKE
QUETSCHEKUCHE

The plum harvest begins in July. The resulting prunes (Zwetschgen – called Quetsche in Frankfurt) herald the prune-cake season.

FOR 1 BAKING SHEET:

DOUGH:
3 ⅓ c flour
1½ oz yeast
1 c milk
½ c butter
2 eggs
½ t salt
Zest of ½ lemon

TOPPING:
1-1½ lb prunes
⅓ c sugar
Cinnamon to taste

PREPARATION:
Place the flour in a bowl, make a well in the center, crumble the yeast into it and pour a little lukewarm milk onto the yeast to dissolve it. Sprinkle the yeast with a tablespoon of the flour, cover and allow to rise in a warm place 15 minutes. Melt the butter and add the remaining lukewarm milk, eggs, salt and lemon zest. Add this mixture to the flour mixture and, using a wooden spoon, stir until the dough pulls away from the sides of the bowl. Place the dough in a warm place and allow to rise again for 15 minutes. Spread the dough on a buttered baking sheet (a jelly-roll pan or

spring form can be used, depending on the desired shape). Wash the prunes and slice them, removing the stones, and arrange, overlapping diagonally, on the dough. Bake in a preheated 425°F oven 45 minutes. Just before serving, sprinkle with sugar and cinnamon. Serve with whipped cream.

DOUGHNUTS

KREPPEL

These doughnuts without holes are served at Carnival time as well as with coffee all year.

SERVES 4:
DOUGH:
2 c flour
½ t salt
¼ c sugar
Zest of ½ lemon
1 oz yeast
1 c milk
2 T softened margarine
2 egg yolks
Oil for frying

ADDITIONS:
Strawberry jam for the filling
Powdered sugar

PREPARATION:
For the dough, mix the flour, salt, sugar and lemon zest in a large bowl. Dissolve the yeast in the milk. Add the margarine, egg yolks and milk mixture to the flour mixture. Knead until smooth. Cover with a cloth and allow to rise at room temperature about 2 hours. When the dough has doubled in volume, form 10 balls of dough. Place on a floured cloth, press a little bit flat and allow to rise again one hour at room temperature. For deep frying, heat the oil in a saucepan or deep-fat fryer to about 400°F. Place 2 or 3 balls of dough at a time – round side down – in the hot oil and cook, covered, about 3 minutes. Turn the doughnuts and

cook another 3 minutes, uncovered. Remove from oil and place on a paper-towel-covered wire rack to drain. Cook all of the dough balls in this way. Place the strawberry jam in a pastry bag, push the point into the warm doughnut and fill the inside with the jam. Dust the doughnuts with powdered sugar. They taste best served warm.

DEEP-FRIED APPLE RINGS
ÄPPELRÄNZSCHER

This is simply apple slices dipped in a beer batter, deep fried and served with a sweet brandy sauce.

SERVES 4:
2¼ lb tart apples, sliced
Juice of 2 lemons
1 T rum
⅓ c sugar
1 lb clarified butter
Cinnamon sugar

BEER BATTER:
1½ c flour
1 pinch salt
1 T sugar
1 c beer
2 egg yolks
¼ c butter, melted
2 egg whites

BRANDY CREAM SAUCE:
1 c cream
1 T sugar
¼ c brandy

PREPARATION:
To make the beer batter, mix the flour, salt and sugar in a bowl. Stir in the beer. Add the egg yolk and luke-warm butter. Mix well and allow to sit 30 minutes in a warm place. Beat the egg whites until stiff and fold into

the batter. Peel and core the apples and slice into circles about ½-inch thick. Coat immediately with the lemon juice. Place the apple slices in a bowl with the rum and sugar to marinate. Heat the clarified butter in a deep saucepan to 350°F. Dip the apple slices into the beer batter, shaking off the excess, and cook in the hot clarified butter. As soon as the undersides turn golden brown, turn the pieces and cook until the other side also turns golden brown. Remove from the pan and drain on paper towels. Coat both sides with cinnamon sugar. For the sauce, beat the cream until firm but not stiff. Add the sugar and brandy. Serve the apple slices with the brandy cream.

Apple-Wine-Pub „Adolf Wagner"

Recipe Index

Linda White
born in Corinth, Mississippi, USA has lived in Frankfurt am Main almost 30 years. She began cooking at the age of 4, standing on a chair to learn from her mother and grandmother. After a stint as Travel Editor of The Stars & Stripes, European Edition in Darmstadt, she stayed in Germany to work as a freelance journalist. She has written a number of travel- and food books.

Evert Kornmayer
born in 1965 in Bensheim on the Bergstrasse, is the author of cook- and specialized books, a hobby cook and gourmet. He lives near Frankfurt am Main. During his many travels within- and outside Germany, he has accumulated extensive knowledge about countries and their kitchens. These experiences and collections are the basis for his culinary work, which includes more than a dozen cookbooks. Two of them are about the Frankfurt kitchen. Prizes & awards: Gourmand World Cookbook Award 2008 „Best Culinary Travel Guide" / Gourmand World Cookbook Award 2005 „Best french cuisine book" / Gourmand World Cookbook Award 2005 „Special Award of the Jury" „best book trade magazines for cookbooks" / Gourmand World Cookbook Award „Best Cookbook Author in the World".